Even executives and managers must be able to talk to others. Communication is truly and genuinely vital to creating and running a successful business. Good communication includes good conversation. Good conversation is about expanding and heightening what is between you and the other people in the room. There is a time for a good yarn and there are people who love to hear about your vacation, but keep it to a minimum. Follow the rules of good conversation. Avoid such questions as "How was your weekend?" Don't start conversations with "I": "I think Kennedy was killed by the CIA and here is why ... Blah, blah, blah." A negation has many forms. Do not negate. But do read this book for good ideas, including how to improvise your conversation in and around the office.

IMPROV FOR EXECUTIVES

Robin G Brown

Published by Free Speech Press
Sierra Vista, Arizona 85635

ISBN:9798389175648

Acknowledgments

I would like to thank Noelle, Amir, Samantha, Arnaud, and all the other people whose advice I ignored.

Introduction

I am constantly asked why I haven't written a book. I usually explain that I am a teacher and a lecturer. I am a public speaker. I tell stories and anecdotes to make a point.

Then an associate suggested that I just tell a story.

He mentioned the story of a very successful case history that I have used at lectures for several years. Why not write that story?

That was my in; I didn't have to write a textbook, all I had to do was tell a story. This is that story.

"We have shared a high endeavor; we have witnessed scenes of beauty and grandeur; we have built up a lasting comradeship among ourselves and we have seen the fruits of that comradeship ripen into achievement."

– Sir John Hunt, head of the British expedition on being the first team to reach the peak of Mt. Everest.

Part One: Improv

Networking is the lifeblood of business. Building rapport with clients and co-workers is essential for success. This book is about improving your ability to speak comfortably and charismatically in all business environments, formal and informal. Whether it is with clients, co-workers, and peers, or superiors. This is *entirely* contingent upon learning the basic rules of improvisation and then applying them in both social and more-structured business situations. It is about how *building rapport* through humor can help achieve better results in the workplace.

Improvisation, whether done in troupes or by individuals, is about extemporaneous intercourse. It is about riffing. I believe business discourse can benefit from the rules that improvisers and comedians use on stage. We will learn how to "riff," or continue a conversation, how to be better at taking criticism, and how to use the basic rules of improvisation to become more comfortable in every social situation. Then we will discuss specific situations: the first meeting, opening and closing a meeting, presentations, brainstorming, job interviews, "elevator chatter," meeting with a famous person, dating, and see how applying these rules can improve performance by removing social anxiety.

Good improvisation is predicated on two basic philosophies and a few general rules: "Get out of your imagination and into the circumstances," "expand and heighten," avoid questions, don't negate, and stay away from starting a sentence with "I." These are the tenets taught at The Second City Theater in Chicago where Del Close groomed a generation of great improvisers: John and Jim Belushi, Andy Dick, Mike Myers, and I among them. The skills we learned there can easily be transferred onto the business stage.

What is meant by "get out of your head and into the circumstances"? In the improv sense, it means we cannot see what is in your head unless you tell us, whereas we can see what is in the circumstances between us. It is shared. This is why in improv we have the rule No imaginary animals. Why is that? Because if you put an imaginary dog in the room between improvisers you have a group of people seeing a different dog doing different things, because the dog is not in the circumstances between them – it is in their imaginations.

The only way we can explain what the dog is doing is to go into our imagination to tell everyone, and let's face it – being told something is not conversation. In theater that is what is called expository dialogue. Expository dialogue is the death of all drama and in the business world it is likened to a PowerPoint presentation. Any time you are telling us something you are in your *imagination* – no one can see your dog, so don't tell us about it.

When something is in the circumstances, we all know about it. We have all seen the latest Academy Award-winning movie or we all went to Athens on a business trip or we are all aware the new factotum is the boss's son. These things are in the circumstances that we all share; we may never have met your children, may not have seen the opera *Les Miserables* – and telling us about it does it no justice. We may not care one hoot about your conspiracy theories. If these things are not shared, then they are not in the circumstances of conversation – they are in your head. To talk about them comes from your imagination, not the things we all share. Conversation by definition is an informal exchange of ideas by spoken words, an exchange – not a monologue.

If you bring up something in a conversation make sure that what you are talking about is familiar to most of the people present. That is what is meant by being in the circumstances. Try it on people. It might be difficult at first, especially if you have a tendency to use every conversation to talk about your kids or your theories on the 9/11 disaster, or, worse yet, if you always speak of the day's work travails. We all know this person. If it is you, you have taken the first step by reading this book, and you are now on the road to fixing that.

We all know good storytellers and often will spend an entire coffee break listening to a yarn about the guy they just swindled. But that is not conversation. That is storytelling, a monologue, and is generally not a good thing to do in a business situation where there are several people around, especially on a golf course or after work having drinks. No one wants to be trapped in the middle of a story that never ends.

Try to stick to anecdotes. A story about your rental car spinning out in the rain the first time you drove in Los Angeles will lead others in the room to tell similar tales, each expanding on the last until it is played out. It might end up being about damaging rental cars, driving in the rain, or how bad the traffic is in Los Angeles.

Storytelling is especially bad in job interviews. Have you ever been in an interview and the human resources person is looking at his watch while you try to finish the story of why you want to sell annuities for a living? Or, how your father taught you honesty on the golf course, *as opposed to the ones that end with you and that interviewer laughing about all the idiots you have both known who have no idea how to putt?* You find yourself getting up and impersonating crazy putting stances, while the other interviewees are waiting outside wondering what the hell is going on in there. That is a job you have already won; all you had to do was look around the room at all the miniature golf course trophies. *Talk about what is shared.*

Unless you are very clever and lead a fascinating life or are a total buffoon, no one wants to hear you recount going to the hospital with a sick child, no one wants to hear your day's travails. It is the modern version of showing vacation slides. Good conversation is discussing something that is shared by everyone in the conversation. It is the fodder for discussion. Mention that someone needs to switch to decaf. A coffee comment is amusing as it implies that someone is talking too much. Talk about the office Halloween party that you all attended, or how the boss drones on in meetings, or start to mimic how he says *vis-à-vis* in every sentence, how someone forgot it was dress down Friday, or the flower labels on someone's food in the fridge. Look for things that are shared, they are the best things to riff on.

Yes, and ...

"Yes ... and" continues a discussion. The "yes" is an agreement, the "and" is something added on to heighten it. Expand and heighten is the nature of improv. Each gem of conversation you receive you should attempt to develop and strengthen. You are adding to the conversation and helping it build into a riff. A good riff can last an entire round of golf, all the way to the nineteenth hole and beyond ... It can even be continued on the next round. It becomes a game in itself, shared by only those of you who were there. And, yes, it generally means making fun of someone or something. Have you ever seen a comedian who is not making fun of someone or something? (Usually about himself and/or his family.) This sort of self-deprecating humor is a good way to take a ribbing. Saying yes and then expanding on it always turns it back on the criticizer, and gets a laugh rather than starting an argument. I will get into how to take a ribbing in greater detail later on in the chapter.

A bond forms when everyone has a shared laugh, and each time they revisit it they are reconvening members of a club. They are sharing a common past. They are replaying a game where only they know the rules. Everyone wants to be in the club. And the only way to bring in a new member is to revisit the riff. That is what a comedy routine is, revisiting a riff about something – the government, family members, dating. What happens when a group of people goes together to see a comedian? They spend days revisiting the funniest riffs. This is *Team Building*. Short of surviving a harrowing experience, nothing builds camaraderie like a good laugh.

Let's begin with the opening line in a conversation when nothing has previously been discussed on which to expand. How does one start a great conversation? Knowing what is shared is key. Anything can get one started. The privileges that the boss' son enjoys or perhaps the boss' disillusionment as to his son's skill set can provide endless anecdotal incidents to continue a riff. As we will soon see, making fun of someone, or *ribbing,* can provide endless riffs.

We all know the one person who hates being ribbed or ridden. We pull her chain intentionally to get her goat. Trust me, if you were an improviser in my hometown of Chicago and everyone knew that you were quick to get on a soapbox, they would find some way to pull your chain, to get you started on a diatribe. If you are this person, the key is not to get angry. The key is to turn it into a riff. Agreement deflects criticism.

Good humor comes from the *reversal of expectation*. When you find yourself cringing and becoming defensive, then, instead of arguing, agree and add to it. Reverse the expectation that you will be defensive by instead agreeing. Try to be self-deprecating. It shows that you are not so insecure that you can't make fun of yourself. Self-deprecation is a great quality to have and is the beginning of humor. In light social conversation, try to keep your axes hidden. There is a time and a place for that, although no one really wants to hear it anyway. When you hear a comment about you, never deny it. Expand on it. Try it some time. You will find that you can turn a comment that makes you uncomfortable into a good laugh. If someone asks you if you washed your hair recently, say, "yes, the first of every month, like clock-work." Try not to rebuff but rather deflect with agreement and get a laugh instead.

Let's visit a real workplace then breaking down the common conversational *faux pas*. A good improv opening line includes the who, what, and where. The famous scene at Second City with Del Close and Phyllis Diller is a great example.

He said, "Honey, put the kids to bed; we are late for the movie."

This line includes the relationship, the place and time in their lives, and the action.

In the same way a good opening line in social conversation might be, "Jan loves an occasional night out without the kids." The implication (subtext) being that she parties too much. This directed at Jan might be taken wrong if she is uptight about her late-night habits. She might get defensive.

Now, how might an uptight Jan handle this? Her reply would generally be either an insult. "Dan is just jealous that he can't stay in a relationship long," or an outright denial: "I do not." Both are what we call *negations*. Jan is "negating" the onward flow of the discussion. She is not saying *yes, and ...* , adding to the conversation. The best way to deal with being ribbed is to agree with it by expanding upon it. Negations end communication. ***Do not negate!* Rule number one.**

How might she diffuse this humorously, and continue the conversation or "riff"? Easy. Now comes the "*Yes, and ...*" part. She could say, "You don't know my kids," meaning that they are a handful – if she wanted to *play against expectation* and get funny. Of course she loves her kids and is a good mom. In social conversations the "truth" is not important. Agree to anything. See how many laughs you get.

Reversal of Expectation is at the heart of all humor. The expectation is, sure, she loves her kids and thinks they are darlings, but the nature of humor is reversal of expectation. Henny Youngman's line is a classic example: "Take my wife, please."

Reversal of expectation is also a good opening line. It has all three, who, what and where, and it's funny. Wouldn't Del Closes's line have been funnier if he had reversed the expectation that he set up? "Honey put the kids to bed, I want to spend more time with the baby sitter."

That is funny because it is a reversal of what you expect. You expect that they would be going to see a movie. You don't expect that he is sleeping with the babysitter.

Dan is single, sarcastic, listens to ABBA, and likes musicals. Everyone in the office kids him about being gay. He could shoot back with, "That's why I don't have any kids," when Jan said that they were a handful. And she could say, "You have to have a girl-friend to have kids." And so on. Now we have a riff going. If Dan were to say, "I can have a kid with my husband" when Jan suggested that he would have to have a girlfriend, that would be even funnier because it is a reversal. He is agreeing to the ribbing that's been dished out about his sexuality and expanding upon it. Admitting to it is funny and a good way to remove social tension, to deflect. Does it matter whether he is gay or not? No. See how the *yes* is implied? *Yes*, that is why I don't have any. Or *Yes*, I'm gay. A negation is the opposite of *yes* ... *and*. Again, do not negate.

A *negation* can come in many forms. A negation can simply be a *no* or a denial. We all know people who use every conversation as an excuse to go into their imagination and tell something that is on their mind. This, too, is a negation. Again, this is in their head. It is a negation of a social conversation, as this person is not expanding and heightening what is between everyone. They are looking for a reason to talk about their financial woes, or their anger over not being promoted, or their health issues, and they will always find a way to segue into one of their *monologues*. If this is you, try to listen and stay in the conversation.

A negation is often funny, but it is at the expense of the riff. When Del said to Phyllis to put the kids to bed, her response was a negation. According to him she said, "We don't have any kids," and got a huge laugh at the scene's expense. The riff was over. As legend has it Del walked off the stage and Phyllis became a stand-up comedian because she didn't play well with others. She didn't *riff,* she stole the scene. A riff is *the goal of social conversation* and it is the key to building humor to the point where everyone is laughing out loud.

A poor opening line usually begins with the personal pronoun "I" because using this word often leads you into your head and out of the circumstances. If you find yourself beginning with "I" you are generally about to regurgitate how much you know about finance or what you think about gun control or, worse, what happened to you that day. Zach might say, "I have to go to the doctor again today." Then everyone sips coffee and hopes he doesn't continue. "I" is usually followed by "think." Anything you think is, duh, in your head. *No personal pronouns!* **Rule number two.**

Dan might say, "The musical numbers were great." rather than, "I think the musical numbers were great," and then explain why he thought so. Taken as an opening line this might become a funny riff in the break room, self-deprecating humor. Dan is *yes ... and*ing to the ribbing that he is gay. Jan could take that and add, "And didn't you just love the gowns?" even though everyone knows she didn't watch. If she were in her negation mode she would say, "I don't have time to watch TV" – a negation in the sense that it ends the riff. You can't get hung up on what is the real truth if you want to riff. Self-deprecation is one of the most endearing of human qualities but it requires a little bit of deflection, a little bit of fibbing.

When a riff gets started, it is everyone's job to add to it until it can be brought around to some final, funny, summation line or conclusion. The young hip girl, Cathy – who tries too hard to fit in, might add, "The opening number was tits." Now the riff can go any direction. What we are doing now is what Del calls *finding the game within the game*. What game are we playing in this riff? Is it about the Grammys? Dan's sexuality? Jan's burning the candle at both ends? It often goes off on tangents.

Now Dan could not let this go: "Why is 'tits' good and 'dick' negative?"

Jan: "He's right: dick is negative."

Dan: "I think we should coin the idiom, 'dick' is a good thing. 'Dick' means 'cool'."

The office factotum, Ben, now knows the game within the game when he adds, "That idea is dick," and everyone laughs.

Dan: "I think this coffee is dick."

The stiff boss chimes in with "Beyoncé is dick."

Everyone groans. Dan has to explain that, "A guy is not 'tits' and a girl is definitely not 'dick'."

Everyone laughs and goes back to work. The rules of the game have been established. A riff like that can work for weeks as everyone starts using dick" in place of "great." Free lunches are dick. Payday is dick. And so on until it runs its course. Everyone in the office wants to be in on the joke. Everyone wants to be in the club.

In Hollywood there is an adage: "Everyone wants to be second." What this means is that first is too soon (and often financially risky), and third is too late, it is already played out. "Dick" will eventually get played out and the game will end. Except for the boss who catches on too late and when he starts calling everyone's work "dick" and all he gets are groans.

How we know something is played out takes

playing and being in the circumstances, but when it starts getting groans it is usually over. The goal in a riff is to bring it full circle before it gets played out. This one ended when someone said that the Rolling Stones' show the previous night was *really* tits – taking tits back from dick once and for all.

Asking a question is usually not good social conversation either. Try turning it into a pronouncement instead. Avoid asking people questions that lead them to regurgitating what is in their heads. *No questions.*

Questions almost always lead the person out of the circumstances and into their imagination. And that can lead to a long explanation of how pi was derived or, worse, the day's activities. Don't ask. At least after wading through the pi explanation you have something to tell your kids. Listening to someone's day is a useless waste of time. If you are one of these people, stop it, **now**. No one wants to hear that your parking meter wasn't expired, or how the landlord is not fixing the leak above your toilet. This is not conversation. I don't know what it is. Chitchat? Kvetching?

Now, I'll do a little explaining, just to demonstrate how clever I am. Do you know where the word scuttlebutt came from? A scuttlebutt was the fresh water barrel on old ships. That is where people met to drink water, and kvetch, chitchat, and, among the clever, riff. This might be a good anecdote to open a riff. "I bet everyone laughed at Captain John Cook's jokes." "I bet he was a great raconteur." As an exercise try to continue my riff about Captain Cook. "But don't ask him about the hook!"

"Yeah, the last guy that did was 'One Eye'."

"I heard he wipes his butt with the left."

"If he ever breaks the other hand *you'll* be wiping his butt …"

The point is, if you are the one who explained how pi was derived it came out of your imagination and the only reason you said it was to prove how smart you are. If you are that smart, you don't need to talk about it. Again the only reason to tell an anecdote is to start a riff.

When the question was asked earlier, "Why is *tits* good and *dick* bad?" it lead the conversation into a game. But as a conversation starter a question almost always leads a person to become didactic. No one wants to hear a speech over coffee or out on the golf course. But hell, you asked them how the dental work went. It's your fault. *No questions!* **Rule number three.**

Most people who ask questions do it because somewhere along the way, whether in a book or at the direction of another teacher, they were told that it was good to ask questions – that it showed you were a caring person, or whatever. Try to use questions judiciously, knowing that they generally lead to meaningful conversation.

So now we have the three rules of improv or riffing and the core principles.

1. *No negations*
2. *No personal pronouns*
3. *No questions*

Get out of your imagination and into the circumstances – expand and heighten! Try it and see how much better the conversation goes. I have been using it on dates for years and went from someone who talks too much about himself to someone who makes my date laugh, much better for casual conversations! Save the life experiences, goals, and attitudes for after dinner.

Part Two: Personality Types

People fall into personality habits unconsciously, over time. Breaking those habits takes conscious effort and practice. Now that we understand the basic tenets of improvisation, the second part of learning to be better at conversation is to understand what type of person you are, seeing how it might be impairing your ability to succeed, and practicing the necessary changes.

Since you have read this far, let's assume you want to change. In the next two sections we will examine typical conversational *faux pas* and show a case history of how a group of coworkers who were "conversationally challenged" changed into conversational experts. In so doing, they achieved much greater success in their careers.

I have broken it down into six specific conversational types that I have found in my research, my own experiences lecturing, work-shopping, and socializing:

- Raconteurs
- Uptight and Defensive
- Shy
- Chatty
- "Monologuers"
- "Regurgitaters"

Obviously, we can all be parts of each at any moment. Being in improvisation my whole life I have known many people who riff way too much. They are always "on" and looking for the next riff, at the expense of *any* meaningful conversation. As I said earlier, there is a time for meaningful conversation and a time for riffing. I had a friend once say, of a famous deal-maker, "We spend fifty-five minutes laughing and five minutes closing the deal." That is a high ratio, but you get the joke – more riffing, less meaningful conversation.

Do you talk about yourself too much?

Start out by paying attention. That means getting out of your head and whatever you are fixating on and becoming present. If there are six people in the break room and you are talking more than a sixth of the time you are talking too much. Try listening and then *yes, and*. Try being the person who starts the riff, not one who starts the conversation. I had that problem when I was younger – always trying to initiate the scene, always wanting people to follow me. I thought I was clever and had the cleverest things to say in the room. Del told me that from now on I was to follow. I was never to start a scene. My only job was to *expand and heighten* something someone else had said, to make them look good. It was hard at first. But I did it and I am, as a result, a much better date, at least. Try to incorporate what Del Close told me into your daily conversations.

Are you worried that you have nothing clever to say?

Some people are intimidated and afraid to join in the conversation. They do not want to be put on the spot. They are afraid they will have to tell a funny story or admit that they believe a 727 took out the tower at the World Trade Center. They sit back in their own imaginations afraid to jump into uncharted circumstances. Misty is one of these. She was in the break room for the "dick" riff, but she added nothing. She wanted to say she did like the musical numbers at the Grammys but was afraid she would be ridiculed for always siding with Dan. She doesn't quite understand that her real opinions are not the point. She wanted to defend Dan because she has a not-so-secret crush on him. She wonders why he would let people say those things about him. She did not know how to *expand and heighten*. She understood that Dan is not gay, but she didn't understand that he was just trying to be funny. She did not realize that how you really feel about the Grammys has no relevance at all. She did not understand that all that matters is saying *yes, and …*

If she had any conversation skills at all she could have said at some point, "Dan is dick and he likes musicals." *Musicals are "tits" not "dick"* being the riff. People are starting to rib her about having a crush on him. Expanding on one's own foibles is always a good way to get a laugh, and that wins people over. ***Agree*** in order to deflect criticism. People cannot pull your chain if you don't let them. It might have been the first time that Dan actually paid any attention to Misty. And *he* would bear the brunt of the laughter. And surely that riff would continue for a while. Dan would start being called "tits" and would not have heard the last of Misty's crush on him from everyone. Now that is a long way for Misty. She must practice riffing outside of the office, around people with whom she is more comfortable. If Misty is you, your first exercise is to do just that: ***expand and heighten*** every criticism you receive. See how long it takes you to get a laugh. See how good it feels. Gain confidence from that.

We can all be defensive at some point, so we should all learn the benefits of agreeing in order to deflect a jibe or a criticism. In my experience, there is no better way to gain friends and influence people than being good at taking a jibe, spinning it into self-deprecating humor. Humility is a strong characteristic, not a weak one.

No matter what your dominant personality type is, practice agreeing, even if the comment is rude and wrong, nay, *especially* if it is rude and wrong. ***Yes, and ... expand and heighten***. Find people who know the rules and play with them. They are usually the center of attention. Hang out together. Laugh together. Jibe. Give this book to someone else. Form a club where riffing is the game. When you sit around in a restaurant or breakroom laughing your ass off with friends and coworkers, people take notice. They want to be in the club. Everyone wants to be in on the joke. This builds rapport.

Do you dominate conversations?

Dan is usually funny at telling stories but spends too much time dominating conversation. Dan is a **Raconteur**. Dan dresses like he was raised in the Hamptons – khakis and navy jackets mostly, with expensive soft-soled brown leather shoes that look as if he could

wear them in the America's Cup final. On dress-down Fridays, he concedes to just a cable sweater but wears it exclusively over his shoulders. Dan enters the break room already talking, he negates whatever private chitchat is going on, and although he usually brings the whole room together, he then dominates all conversation. One anecdote leads to another and on many days he has people laughing, but it is at the expense of conversation. He hardly knows anyone in the office. I think Dan considers Misty a really attractive young woman and she actually likes him. She dreams about spending romantic dinners listening to him. They are a perfect match. But Dan hardly knows her name because he hasn't spent more than a minute listening to her in six months. Dan's first exercise is to listen and follow, *expand and heighten*. Any social situation he enters, he should make sure that what he says adds to the conversation and doesn't lead him into his head to recount something. He should practice whenever he is in social or business situations, and especially while dating.

Are you uptight and defensive?

Jan is Uptight and Defensive. She does not like being ribbed, so she is an easy mark for ribbing. She wears bright colored skirts and frilly white blouses. She rarely wears a jacket and she hates dress shoes so she wears sneakers to her desk and then slips on pumps. On dress down Fridays she wears black tennis shoes and jeans, but always the blouse. She is the mother of three and juggles it all while being the highest grossing salesperson in the office. She takes everything she does seriously, whether it is raising her kids, working, or going out dancing. She really has no friends in the office, mostly because she is uncomfortable in light conversation. She has never been considered funny, and until the office went together on a mandatory outing she had never even seen a live comedian. She needs to practice deflecting with agreement every time someone pulls her chain. But she does everything seriously so she took the advice in this book seriously. She would not have read it if she hadn't wanted to change, so hers is a tough road. It takes a lot of practice to break down years of defensiveness.

Are you shy?

Misty is Shy. She judges herself too harshly and always worries about whether she is saying the right thing. She dresses conservatively in dark suits and slacks. Her only concession to fashion is her high heels, which she wears as if she had been practicing for the role of businesswoman her whole life. On dress-down Fridays she wears light dresses, but always below the knees. She works through many of her breaks, not because she puts so much pressure on herself, but because she is afraid to venture in when there is a lot of laughter. She has a crush on Dan, mainly because she likes all the things he talks about. She tries endlessly to catch him alone in the break room and have a conversation about award shows or the opera, but is afraid to speak up when other people are around. She needs to try riffing in smaller conversations around people with whom she is more comfortable. Dinner conversations with old friends, around close family, and especially in public situations like commuter trains, elevators, and doctors' waiting rooms, where there are no stakes.

Are you trying to be funny all the time?

Ben tries too hard to fit in. He is a "Monologuer." He has a tendency to try to say funny things from his imagination, jokes, and anecdotes he has heard or read about that day. Ben wears black jeans and black tennis shoes and a black T-shirt in the mail-room. When he makes the rounds, because he thinks it's funny, he pulls on the reflector vest that he is supposed to wear when he is operating the fork-lift truck, as if pushing a cart around required safety clothing. Dan sticks his smartphone in people's faces and forces them to watch "funny" videos every time he delivers a package or collects outgoing mail. That is the reason he is OK to be around on the golf course – phones are against the rules. He talks about video game releases and great porno sites (which is fine on the golf course, unless you are in mixed company). He is the first one to Google something to check their facts. He often talks over people and does not listen well. Ben needs to learn to **expand and heighten** what is being said, what is in the circumstances, and not try to make a joke out of everything he can think of. He riffs with himself when no else will join him. He needs to make other people look good by expanding on what is being said. If he could just sit back a little more and remain in the conversation long enough, he would come up with more funny lines like, "That idea is 'dick'."

Are you always talking about yourself and your own foibles?

Zach always talks about the same things that are bothering him and often repeats anecdotes. He is a "Regurgitator." Zack wears the same army fatigues and steel-toed combat boots every day. The only thing he changes is the heavy metal T-shirt he wears. I am sure he takes a full half-hour deciding which one to wear each day. He plays bass in a cover band on weekends. He claims that is why he dyes his long hair from time to time. Zach often hears comments like, "You already told me that." He has these rants about how computers make everything more complicated and health insurance is a scam and gasoline prices are killing him and his pre-owned car has been in the shop three times already, and the sailboat that he bought a third of is never available on weekends and – his real go-to rant – how he is treated unfairly salary-wise compared to the sales force. He needs to pay more attention and trust that he does not need to hold onto what he is thinking, let it go and wait. Get into the circumstances, *expand and heighten.* Try not to use every opportunity he can find to tell people about all the stuff that is bothering him. If you are in your head waiting for your turn to regurgitate then you are not present. Zach needs to be more present. And he too needs to try to let others get the laugh. I have seen many guys like Zach try to change. It is hard at first. They do a lot of biting their lips, starting to go on a rant then realizing that is not good and stopping themselves. It takes time. Zach needs to realize that social conversation is about humor. Someone needs to tell him.

Do you talk about trivial things too much?

The final type is Chatty Cathy. She is constantly talking and not listening. She wears vintage skirts and frilly shirts with lace collars in light pastel colors. Her jewelry is antique and she wears a lot of it. Lace-up boots, cream colored, usually. She does not dress down. Cathy likes to corner people and have deep discussions one on one, on things like the food in Central America, and her opinion of that comedian they saw, or that Jan's black shoes are tennis shoes. She especially likes to gossip about everyone and everything that is going on in the office. She warns Zach that the shipping department is soon to be computerized, which leads Zack into his "computers are making the world more complicated" speech. That is a conversation no one wants to be in. If she were paying any attention she would realize that Zach likes her. But I could not imagine her dreaming about listening to him over a candlelit dinner - a late-night dinner after a show, maybe. She is a classic negator, because she is always talking and no one else has a chance to get a word in edgewise. She negates everyone else's input. She cuts people off. She cuts Zach off in the middle of his computer rant, but he doesn't care. He is just happy that she is talking to him and he loves to hear dirt about the front office. Cathy often finds that most people are not listening. And she does not care because she likes the sound of her own voice. She is nervous and somewhat insecure. Cathy needs to listen as well. She needs to slow down and get into the circumstances. The Chatty Cathys of the world are the hardest to reach because in order to change they have accept that there is a problem.

In Summary

The first step to "improv-ing" is figuring out which of these people is most like you and then making the right adjustments. If you ask too many questions, work on not asking questions. Work on listening then adding on to what is said. Many people feel that questions are good for conversation, as we have discussed, unless they are the punch line they are usually **not** good for riffing. They are good for getting people to go into their heads and telling you about oral surgery or some other non-scintillating subjects.

If you always talk about yourself try to stop using personal pronouns. If you find yourself saying 'no' a lot and denying, then you need to begin with yes. If you are defensive you need to learn to agree and then add on to that agreement. If you say 'no' as merely an extension, it's a habit. Work on breaking it. If you are afraid to jump into a riff, practice it in more comfortable social situations. If you want people to think you are clever, stop telling stories, try following, waiting for some comment that gets you out of your head and into the circumstances, riff on what they are saying. In each case, try to get out of your imagination and into the present circumstances.

Part Three: Finding the game within the game

"Always forgive your enemies. Nothing annoys them more." – Oscar Wilde

We all agree that in order to get a good riff going we need to get into the present circumstances. Only then can we look for the *game within the game*. The earlier discussion was about the Grammys and Dan's being chided for liking musicals. The game within the game ended up being about "tits" vs. "dick." Think of it this way: in any conversation you are involved in, you should be looking for the thing to riff on, the ***game within the game***, finding the game within the conversation.

With 'dick' now being played out, we should all be looking for the next riff. It might come from a discussion of the Grammys as our "dick" riff did. Or an observation of the way someone is dressed. What is it about human nature that makes most of us uncomfortable when told we look nice in a particular suit or a dress? "Thank you," comes out insincere. "Is that new?" almost always get a, "No, I've had it for a while." How about, "Yes, and thanks for noticing. I spent a fortune on it." More often than not we **negate** by saying something to the extent that we always dress like that or that they have seen that dress before and so on. Are those jeans new? Is that a new suit? Inevitably we claim it's not new or that we've had it for years. We **negate**.

So when Dan says to Misty that she looks nice in a short dress – as opposed to asking, "Is that a new dress?" – he is calling Misty out. He has been paying attention to her lately and has assumed correctly that she wore the dress because she heard him riffing about how he was a leg man when they were talking "tits." I believe he did chide her at the time for always wearing below-the-knee suit dresses. The fact is he just said it to be funny, anyway; I am sure Dan likes tits just fine.

This kind of subtle ribbing happens all the time. We all need to get better at taking it and giving it back.

After a beat Misty recovers and says, "Yes, *I* like to keep up with the latest fashions." She is making a comment on his "classic" New England attire – saying he is behind the times. Wow, she has been practicing. Now she is flirting! That is what someone who likes someone should do. She is dying for Dan to ask her out, but she has not had the courage to say a word to him since she was hired six months ago. Now Dan is up to bat. Can he expand and heighten that? Dan says, " 'Classic' is the new 'trendy'." Misty laughs and asks "Is that so?" Then they have *that* uncomfortable moment, created by Misty's question. A question that begets really only one answer and that is *yeah, that's so*. Avoid these and all polite questions people usually ask, especially *how are you?* in all its forms: *What's new? What's up? Hey?* Instead, say something that is in the circumstances, like Dan's *"Nice Dress."*

Dan says finally "That's so, and especially on a date." Oh, nice, Dan; ball is in your court, Misty. "I like Italian," says Misty after a beat. By now Dan is also impressed with her wit, which he never knew she had. "I know the perfect place" is Dan's obvious response. Riff ended. Date forthcoming. Jan enters, as their eyes linger on each other's. Zach enters behind her, "What did I miss?" asks Jan. She is a little defensive when she feels she missed out on something, but as a question it could lead to a riff. Dan says, "We were talking fashion."

Jan gives Dan a gentle ribbing: "That figures; the latest issue of GQ just hit the newsstand." That is getting a little old coming from Jan; clearly the Dan being gay joke has run its course. Misty is now trying to find a place to *expand and heighten.* If she was thinking she could say, "Dan has the same classic style as you." But she chickened out, and Dan ends up saying, "I don't need magazines to tell me what's in style." Ooh, nice dig, Dan. Everyone knows that Jan's desk has a stack of *New Yorker* magazines on it.

But Misty cannot let go of her idea even though the beat has shifted in another direction. When she finally blurts out, "Dan has the same classic style as you." It gets Misty a mean look from Jan. Jan recovers and says, "There is a difference between 'classic' style and old style."

Dan says, "Take Zach for example," and gets a big laugh.

When Ben adds "Please," as in please take Zach away, the laugh builds to uproarious. Zach has many retorts he can say to deflect this humorously but instead he goes on a rant about how Ben could not do his job, nay, no one in the office could. Zack needs to really work on how to take a ribbing.

The next time a riff gets started is when it is learned that a famous movie star has had breast implants. They are still not as large as Jan's as Ben has not so subtly pointed out. "They would need a truss to hold up that much latex," says Jan. Now, coming from her that line is self-deprecating, and gets a laugh. She is agreeing by adding that breasts that size made out of silicone would weigh a lot. Jan ends up looking good whereas had she gotten negative she would have looked bad. Jan is getting better at this, and the fact is she has mentioned before that she feels they are too large is not the point. Humor is the point. Ben blurts out, "Try having another kid; *that* will make them bigger."

Jan has to bail Ben out of his social *faux pas*. She says, "I tried that; that's why I had a third kid." And that gets a laugh. **Yes**, I tried that **and** that's why I had a third. Good one, Jan, laughs all around.

Ben has been practicing as well – he is just young. As a result he tries a little too hard. He adds, "You can get a reduction." Jan laughs and says, "Is that covered in our insurance?" But Zach is still Zach; he is just looking for a reason to talk about his huge medical deduction. He starts in about how breast implants are not covered by insurance and uses it as an excuse to talk about the electrocardiogram that he requested because he didn't believe his acid reflux wasn't a heart condition – and how that is not covered either. He has now read about everything that is covered. Everyone in the room has already heard this before and most disappear into their own imagination and leave the circumstance, most going back to work early because they would rather work than listen to Zach go on about his deductions and acid reflux.

Ben, however, gamely tries to expand and heighten. "Zach, perhaps you are a hypochondriac."

"Trust me, I have real pain. I can't sleep at night."

And off he goes about one of his other major rants, not sleeping well. Which everyone knows is just his excuse for drinking so much. Ben listens intently while Zach details his sleep habits. Ben has to listen because Zach is his boss. No one else does. Had Zach just followed the rules he could have said, "Yes, I am a hypochondriac, and that's not covered either," and gotten a good laugh. Again agreeing with a dig and expanding on it is always the best thing to do when you are being ribbed.

Now, we have a lot of work to do with Zach. If you are like Zach you probably have no idea that people are making fun of you behind your back. You have no idea that what you are doing is turning people off. Zach wonders why he never gets invited out on golf outings. It has nothing to do with the fact that he works in the mail room. He has the lowest handicap in the office. But who wants to spend five hours listening to someone's verbal diarrhea? Zach is left out of most office gatherings and he is sure it because the mail room gets no love. That is what he tells Ben. But Ben is a twenty handicap and he gets invited out and it is not because he is the boss' son. It is because he is better company, more fun to be around, very self-deprecating.

The next day in the break room, Jan opens with, "My tits are off limits." But of course Dan says, "What does your husband think about that?" Now Jan is in full swing. She says, "He's a leg man," and everyone laughs. We are all in the same club today. We start off running because we know the riff. Misty, thinking that she is better at starting conversations, says, after a pause. "So, he's like Dan." Misty's confidence is rising as her attraction to Dan indicates, "Passions have symptoms that cannot be mistaken," to quote Shakespeare. Jan tries not to be defensive, says, "He's a pitcher not a catcher." Dan is quick, asks, "Does he play third base?" Jan, "Yes, he plays it well. Good hands." And everyone laughs again. Now people want to hang out together. They are forming a clique. Is Jan's husband a leg man? I would doubt it, but who cares?

Much of the humor in mixed company is sexual in nature. I chose to add this bit, because it was real. When I worked with this group I never felt like they were holding back. They may even have been pushing it a little on my account. But you need to be careful with not pushing it to sexual harassment. I am sure Jan was a little offended by Ben's jibe, but she handled it well. She may have gone to Ben's father about it later; I don't know. The point is that if you sense that anyone is of-fended you must back off. It is probably a good idea not to go there at all if you do not know everyone in the room well. Harassment has solely to do with the people in the workplace and their limits. For this group, in this area of the country, most of this was not even remotely offensive. There is a thin line between being funny and being offensive. You must try and stay on the right side of it. Especially in high stakes meetings with clients. Follow their lead. Obviously if they choose to meet in a strip club the level of the humor can go low. But if you are going to a 4H meeting, keep it high. Let common sense guide you. Don't be that "off-color" guy who always pushes the limits of what is polite conversation. In many business situations a conversation like this would be off limits. Know whom you are with and what their limits are before you get too off-color. But as we all know these riffs are typical in many offices and social business situations, and especially on the golf course. Such as, "Dude, you just Sally'd that putt." "Never up, never in."

That night everyone decides to get a drink together before heading home, Misty included. Even Zach is invited. What he doesn't realize is that this is a planned intervention. Misty is now feeling like part of the group. She and Dan riff about men and women. How women talk to each other about sex and men never do.

Eventually everyone gets in on it. "Men do not talk about masturbation."

"That is why men are so bad at sex."

"Women compare notes."

"You never hear one boy telling another that he found a new way to stroke himself."

And so on. Eventually the men concede that women are better lovers as a result of talking amongst themselves about sex from an early age. Is this true? Who knows? Who cares?

This conversation goes by so fast that Zach has not had time to find a way into his imagination. No one is talking about doctors or bills, computers or car dealerships, his go-to conversation topics. Finally someone makes the mistake of asking him – maybe feeling that he is left out. "Hey, Zach, did they fix your window?" Zach, "Yeah, but they said it wasn't under warranty. The warranty is from when the car is originally sold." Dan cuts him off before he can get started. "So, you didn't read the warranty before you signed it?" But off Zach goes anyway. Finally someone stops him, hands him my book and introduces me. "Someone in this is just like you, they tell him." Try to stop talking about yourself. No one wants to hear about your anxieties. They go on to explain to him the real reason I have been watching them for the past few weeks.

Which is why I set these programs up this way. The national director of marketing hired me after he had seen my workshop on building rapport at a leadership conference. The sales force members were told that I am observing them for a screenplay I was writing about a typical office, and that I wanted it to be real authentic, not like "The Office." I told them to act natural and pretend I was not there. I informed them that I was not going to tape them. I usually try to begin in the break room where everyone is together three times a day. I ask them to bring their lunch, or order-in but not go out for lunch. Other than that I observe them in a natural situation long enough for me to get to know them and for them to get comfortable with my being there and to act natural. Then, when I am ready, I meet with them all one by one during work on Friday and give them my evaluation. In this particular group, it was their unanimous idea that I use our parting drinks as an intervention rather than speak with Zach privately.

Zach is sensitive and at first this hurts.

"The first thing is agreement," Jan informs him.

"Try it," says Ben.

Dan notes, "The five things Zach always talks about: His doctors."

"His bills," adds Jan.

"His new car," adds Ben.

Zach counters, "It's used," and Misty explains how that is a negation.

Finally Zach goes along. "Don't forget computers, I always talk about them," and everyone laughs.

Zach now understands. "I won't have anything to say," he jokes.

Everyone laughs and suddenly Zach feels like he is part of the club because he was in on a riff, even if it was at his expense.

I left them to go on the road, but I kept in contact

with the marketing director. He informed me that they began working more closely together to get the orders out and rely on each other to get projects done. Now they were part of the same club – sales, management, shipping department – they were building a great rapport with each other. They hung out together. Suddenly their numbers improved. The team is singled out as exemplary of all the regional offices. The boss thinks this is big "dick," which gets smirks from everyone else. He has this habit of using the word "dick" and making weirdly sexual *double entendres,* which he himself misses, whereas everyone else has avoided those. They start calling him "Big Dick" behind his back.

Each is determined to master the art of conversation. Over the next few months, every chance they get, they riff. Work is fun. Zach remains a work in progress. When his annual review comes up they all coach him. They want to make sure he spends no time complaining about his insurance or his perceived lower status in the mail room.

As Zach tells it, he sits down and listens, just as we suggested. The boss goes on about the coming automation of the shipping department and how Zach will have to learn a few things about computers. He admits to going into his imagination and starting the story he has told a thousand times about why he hates computers. Apparently the boss stopped him mid-sentence. (He read my book before any of them but, sad to say, is still a work in progress.) The boss goes on, "You will be paid for training."

"I hope you have a big budget," Zach says, "It may take a while."

Yes, *and* it may take a while.

The boss laughs, "I guess I should double it." And they both laugh.

I'm sure Zach left the meeting smiling and the boss had a longer lunch that he was expecting.

What if I do have an agenda?

Now, there are times when you do have an agenda. You may be in a meeting and have a few points that you want to discuss, make a sale, get a favor, etc. We will use Cathy as an example. She is the one person in the office who is not up to speed on the rules of conversation. Back from vacation, Cathy can't wait to talk about the monuments of Central America. Cathy needs to learn how to segue. First of all, none of us can tell by flipping through photos on a smartphone that the ocean way in the background is twenty miles on either side, and can be seen from atop Pyramid El Castillo. She needs to wait for an opportunity to come up in conversation where something from her vacation seems a natural extension.

This is difficult, as holding onto something, waiting for an opportunity, means you are not in the circumstance – you are in your head, and as a result you might miss a riff that has nothing to do with how bad the food is in Panama. Or how forward the men are in Mexico, or how a child stole your smartphone, or how everyone walks around without shoes or how the little invisible bugs that bite you in the ocean are called sea lice. Try waiting for these things to come up in conversation.

Wait until someone offers you a vending machine candy before going on about how sick you are of American snack food and how disappointing it was to discover that was all that was available in the jungle. Wait for a mosquito bite before remembering the sea lice, or a conversation about hair lice. Discuss the bare feet thing while everyone is bitching about the new rule about no black tennis shoes at work. And keep the anecdotes short and wait for someone to expand and heighten.

Dan offers Cathy an Oreo. She tells everyone about the food. Dan says, "That's why my idea of a vacation is a four-star hotel." Jan heightens that with a joke of her own, "My idea of a vacation is a good babysitter." Misty adds, "My idea of a good vacation is sleeping under the stars." Zach puts in, "My idea of a good vacation is a world without computers." Ben says, "I don't get a vacation," and everyone laughs. The boss enters and says, "No one is on vacation so get back to work," and everyone goes back to work laughing and invigorated. Isn't that what a coffee break is for? Cathy has had a chance to talk about her vacation without pulling out her smartphone and showing pictures.

It doesn't matter that Misty really hates camping or that Jan likes four-star hotels as well. All that matters is expanding and heightening the riff. Agree to anything. If Jan had said, "I like four-star motels too," it would be a *yes* without the *and*. How about, "How would you know? You have never been to one." That could have sent Dan in a different direction. To agree and reverse expectation he could have added, "I read a lot of brochures." Again he is agreeing. *Yes, and*-ing it. He may have never read a brochure in his life.

The above is an example of a riff on a single phrase, in this case the "my idea of a vacation" phrase. Try one of these on my idea of a good meal, or my idea of relaxation or, my idea of a night out, or a great week-end, and so on. Once you start it will be easy for every-one to chime in on the riff, it may last weeks before it is played out. One of my favorite riffs is dot com names for Pho take-out restaurants: Phoaway.com, Phoout.-com, Pholowme.com, a-pho.com, etc.

Cathy is like Dan: they need to follow. Cathy must remember that there are six people in the conversation not an audience of five. She should probably try the decaf coffee. And people need to give her grief about it as well. Try a time-out mirror where one person holds up the time-out sign until everyone is doing it and she finally gets the point and everyone laughs. That riff led to other referee-style signs, an illegal forward pass when Dan made yet another comment about Misty's legs. Intentional grounding when Ben misses the garbage can with a paper wad by several yards. A touchdown when Jan lands a big account. An incomplete pass when Zach asks Cathy to a show and she says she has plans. Or, out of bounds when Dan sends Misty flowers for Valentine's Day, and so on. Riffs can be on anything. Find the game and you find the riff.

Can a negation be an agreement?

Cathy actually accepts Zach's offer to take her out on a date. She was simply riffing when she said she had plans. How can a "no" still be an agreement?" When she is playing off an existing riff, in this case she is setting up the Illegal Pass signal, and Jan gets it and signals with her hands. Everyone laughs. There is a concept in improv where we agree to disagree. Kind of like a debate competition. Each person could argue either side, and perhaps has a more passionate opinion about second-hand smoke or abortion or whether marijuana is really medicine. These are not really relevant in a scene or a riff. For an argument to be a riff we are agreeing to disagree. Keep looking for riffs – the game within the game. Conversation is not an excuse to argue. If this is you, you are probably not even in the break room. People have already fought with you and you hate them all.

Misty and Dan have a lot in common and, having just watched the Academy Awards, they have something in the circumstances between them to riff on. They have a lovely dinner laughing and rehashing all the moments in the show. They agree to disagree on many of the winners, but mostly they laugh. They leave holding hands. Dan stands at the threshold, trying to avoid the big question, "Can I come up for a nightcap?" He thinks about saying, "I would like to come up" and again stops short of saying "I." Finally he says, "This is where I am supposed to lean in and kiss you." She smiles and he does so. Then she says goodnight and leaves him standing on the stoop.

Dan has a skip in his step as he walks back to his car. Misty is probably leaning her back against the closed door, her heart racing. Ah, isn't love grand? Don't answer that. I don't want to hear it.

Monday at work Misty and Dan do their best not to gloat around the office but by the lunch break when Misty walks into the canteen everyone is abuzz about it. Jan says, "Well, did you use contraception?"

Misty blushes but she is now on her game, she says, "Yes, and rubber gloves."

Instead of taking offense (they did not sleep together) she *Yes, ands*, and gets a big laugh. This goes way back to the "third base" joke. Good job, Misty.

Dan walks in while they are laughing and says,

"Wait a second, did I miss something?"

Cathy says, "Apparently." Now it is Dan's turn to blush.

When he arrives at the canteen in the afternoon, Ben has left a pair of the heavy black cleaning gloves on the table, and the riff is on. Have Misty and Dan had sex? No. But what difference does that make? It is none of anyone's business. To get defensive is not the way to handle that. She did the *yes, and* ... Now everyone is on her side. She has gone from a mouse to a cat in a short time. Her confidence is at an all-time high. All the girls now hang out together whenever Jan can get a babysitter, and I occasionally join them. Jan and Cathy are helpful where before they ignored her. Of course Misty admits, over drinks, that they just kissed. They have fun pulling her chain about her relationship with Dan, making her blush. Clearly she likes Dan a lot and has to work not to be defensive. We have all been through this. We have all had this chain pulled. Remember *yes, and* ... when your chain is being pulled. Cathy states, "You'll have to quit." Misty responds with, "Yes, and he'll need a promotion," implying that she is only going to quit in order to raise children.

I came back on Monday to finish up and ended up spending another day with them. When pried about what happened, Dan was a little more circumspect, but he makes it clear that they are taking it slowly, which, of course, means he takes more ribbing for liking her. But he is prepared to give it back. When asked when he plans to see her next, he pulls a pair of thin rubber gloves out of his wallet just as a young man would a prophylactic he has been carrying around for years. When the boss crosses to see what they are laughing about everyone changes the subject. This is a now a team; no one is going to throw either Dan or Misty under the bus for fraternizing.

How do I practice staying out of my head?

There is an improv game called *Freeze Tag*. Groups of five or more are needed. One person begins and pantomimes an activity, say shoveling snow. As soon as they have recognized the activity the first person to say, freeze, has to replace them in the same position they were frozen in and then transform it into something else. In this case, with the shovel high overhead tossing the snow. When freeze was yelled the shovel was down but by the time Dan froze it was high over his head. If you yelled freeze with an idea how to transform the shovel into a push broom you have to let it go. It is now over your head. You must learn this trick of letting go and trusting that something else funny will come up out of the circumstance. This trust in yourself takes practice. You can't put the shovel back down and do your broom idea.

Assume the position and let the circumstances inform you. With one forward motion the shovel becomes a fishing rod and is cast into the water. At this point someone else yells freeze and by the time he freezes the pole is going back to cast. With a pull back and a snap the pole becomes a whip. And so on. When this is done on stage all the bits are usually coming out of the imagination of the improvisers. That is to say, they are playing things that they have used before that get a laugh. They are not improvising in the real sense; they are playing rehearsed bits out of their imagination. This is an important distinction.

The real point of this exercise is to teach yourself to let go of an idea and trust that another will come as soon as you assume the position. Each person must play on every turn. So if you have a tendency to sit back and not jump in, relax, knowing you are last is the best place for you. With whatever position is frozen you will be forced to get your idea from the circumstances, not out of an idea you have been holding for three turns.

This exercise serves two purposes: Practicing finding a way to get your idea into the conversation, and learning to let go of an idea if the moment passes. Let it go and wait for the next one. When you get to this confidence level you are relaxed and usually a lot funnier. You are always in the circumstances. You are present. I have had people tell me that I am "present." It is the opposite of "absent." I considered it high praise, then I said, "Yes, and I have a book you should read."

Part Four: Case History

The following spring they are all at a conference that I am attending. We hang out together and really bond. Other regional offices take notice. Everyone already knows that their office is outperforming all the others. Now management gets to see why. They are a team and they like each other. They play a little game. Each sits at a different banquet table. They have a bet to see who can get their whole table laughing first. "I'm Emily from Des Moines," a woman offers. Dan jumps right in and expands upon what she said. "Hi, my name is Dan and I'm from Chicago, and my hobbies are skiing and sailing." Unfortunately the next gentleman drops the riff saying. "I can see your name tag," negating the riff about silly introduction exercises before it can get started.

At Jan's table someone offers, "Even the banquet chicken is good in New Orleans." Jan adds, "Yes, and the drinks are strong." Unfortunately, the chuckle she gets from a few is negated when someone asks her how her kids are doing. But she jumps right in, "With their father." And smiles. Now, if just one of the men at the table can take the intended dig in this, that a man's place is in the home, and spin it, we may have a riff going, something to the effect that they don't allow kids in bars or on the golf course would get everyone going on the battle of the sexes and who does a better job of raising kids. The fact is they are with their grandmother, but once again, when riffing no one cares about the facts.

Someone at Cathy's table asks her how her trip to Panama went. She is aware of her tendency to regurgitate and wants to win the bet. She says, "The food sucked, no one wears shoes, and my phone was stolen by a five-year-old." And she gets a laugh. Someone asks her what was wrong with the food. She says, "Nothing if you normally eat at a gas station store." A clever gentle-man adds, "So they have foot-long hot-dogs? I'm there." And he gets a laugh. Cathy adds, "I lived on Oreos for three weeks." A young woman chimes in, "I did that once when I was ten." And now a riff is going. Cathy needs to close it with something that makes the whole table laugh, but she is careful not to get into her head and think about it.

Misty is listening to some woman go on about how the last time she was in New Orleans was on her honeymoon twelve years ago. She is even showing pictures. Misty looks around and sees that at Cathy's table people are laughing. The woman turns to her and says, "Would you like to see them?" How in the hell does one *yes, and* ... that? "Yes, and I'll have another drink," is what I'm thinking. Misty says. "Yes, and I'll buy a wedding book as well." This gets a gentle chuckle from a few of those present. Good one, Misty.

Dan's table has gone off on an unexpected tangent. He has a few managers present and they are drilling him about the office chemistry. He mentions my book and points me out walking around the banquet room. He says things like, *we don't take each other too seriously* and *we like each other*, but falls short of saying that it wasn't always that way. He looks over, as does his whole table, when Cathy's table erupts in laughter. She smiles over at him, having won the bet. After dinner everyone wants to know what was so funny. Cathy explains that she started a riff about bad food snacks and she brought it around when telling the server that she wanted Oreo ice cream for dessert. A reversal of the expectation that she'd had all the Oreos she ever wanted, and as a result she had gotten a big laugh from everyone at the table.

I was invited by the same marketing VP who had hired me and asked to meet with the other offices about doing a similar program. When the managers meet with me I just listen. They discuss how to make people in other offices like our office. A brainstorming session ensues. Things like more picnics, bowling, and comedy nights are proposed. The boss is asked why they are so tight a group and he has his segue. I am introduced. It doesn't go that well. My speech about how riffing leads to rapport falls flat.

Finally, management decides that they should watch his office at work. A task force is formed and dispatched. The following Monday the gang are greeted in the canteen by two management types and me, again. They are told to act natural. Of course the first thing Dan does is stand with his arms crossed like one of the managers. Jan sees it as does Misty and soon everyone is mimicking him. Finally the manager being mirrored gets it and goes on about how hard it will be for them to act natural and just do what they do. When in fact they were acting naturally and doing what they do. Zach and Ben have been asked to take breaks later so that the management team can watch the sales force in action. Zach is mad about it and he has a meeting with the boss about the disrespect the mail room receives; already the team is becoming fractured.

Now, what one can see by my real case is that a

group with these skills will be better able to handle the pressure of being watched than a typical sales team. In fact the situation is ripe for a week of mad riffing. What we have is the expectation of some great bits. This group of managers will be in the circumstance between them. We can see where this might lead. Seeing where something is going is the advanced stuff of improv. If you can see where a riff is going you can look for a conclusion, something to wrap it all up, to bring the entire process to a close and tie everything together, something to get the big laugh. I will attempt to demonstrate.

That afternoon at break the gang is again put together with each other. Having been observed at their desks all day they have not had time to riff while working, which is what they do to pass the drudgery. They cannot wait to meet after work and commiserate, riff on it. But it is unsaid. Jan talks about her kids, and the managers take note. Dan talks about travel brochures, and the managers take note. Cathy talks about her trip to Panama (in detail), and the managers take note. Can you see what they are riffing on? What the game is? The game is that they can't riff right now. Each is playing back to how they used to be. Albeit more cleverly. Dan's line is quite clever because it actually has nothing to do with anything real. He does not read brochures. It is a riff on the riff about "'my idea of a great vacation."

This is the stuff of a good situation comedy, right? I should sell this idea. Wait, "The Office" already did it. Watch "The Office" again and see how the writers expand and heighten a riff. Or "Breaking Bad" – they work the reversal of expectation from concept all the way through each character and each scene to get humor. The idea that a man dying of cancer chooses to sell drugs to pay for the hospital bills is a reversal of expectation. The fact that he is a high school chemistry teacher heightens that, and it also helps the plot because he can easily make methamphetamine. In the second episode you do not expect that that acid filled tub full of decomposing flesh is going to fall through the floor right when a real estate agent is showing the house. The deep truth in each is equally informing. *A man will do anything to save his family* is not exactly a bad theme.

So, over drinks, the group has a chance to decompress. I join them. After Zach is finished explaining how he feels dissed, they realize that Zach went to the boss. "Zach, going to the boss angry is like angry texting. It never comes out the way you think it will," says Dan.

Jan: "Yeah, Zach, not a good idea. You should have gone on strike as a protest."

Ben: "I could handle it for a few days, or until they hired someone else."

Misty: "I would offer to take over the mail room."

Cathy: "We could all take shifts."

But Zach is agro and cannot let go. He holds onto one though – that they could not do his job, and when they are done riffing, ribbing him. He says to Ben, "You could not handle my job. None of you could," and gets up and leaves, they all realize that they have hurt his feelings. They decide that the next day they should show up in the mail room and help Zach as a protest. If the managers wish to see team building they will show them some team building.

The next morning at eight a.m., an hour earlier than usual, they show up in the mail room. By the time the boss and the management team find them they are all laughing as Zach shows each of them how the new system works and each has a go at how complicated it really is. Management could not have come at a better time. They take notes. The group is lauded for their initiative. Exactly the opposite of what they intended. Which is why this situation is funny. Reversal of what you expect. Situation comedy = Sitcom.

They are not sure whether to push the protest when each has had his turn or simply go back to work. It is break time. So they take a break and meet in the canteen. The management team takes notes. Having spent the last two and a half hours riffing, the sales team is spent. Management senses this and everyone is given the rest of the day off as a reward. Not what they expected. Management meets all afternoon; training the other sales teams on the computer is considered a good idea. Each week a salesperson will have to come in and familiarize him- or herself with the new system. Ugh.

Great idea, that is sure to bond all the other sales teams together – against management. That is one way to team build. I doubt it will show an uptick in production. On the contrary, this whole idea is bound to backfire.

They come up with a few team-building initiatives that they would like to implement in each office: weekly bowling after work, mandatory sales staff training on the new shipping system, better food in the canteen.

Can you see the end of the riff coming? What will happen?

By the end of the week the gang has loosened-up. The banter around the office resumes. The management staff takes notes. Friday is usually a busy day, and when someone is looking over your shoulder all the time, you are bound to be more productive. They break a sales record for a week but only after working an hour overtime. Jan throws up the touchdown sign when her sale pushes them over the record. The boss springs for beer and pizza for everyone. Zach and Ben are invited to join in. The boss is thrilled that his team broke the record while upper management was in the house. He gives a speech and uses the term "super dick," and the room breaks up in laughter, and as he stands there, dumbfounded, it grows into a roar. He has no idea of the joke he just made.

Everything is going well until Dan is called into the office. They all fear that he and Misty's relationship has been discovered. When he comes out they are stunned. Management has offered him the sales manager job in Iowa. It is a big promotion but he and Misty are thinking of moving in together. He asks for the weekend to think about it.

Misty listens intently, trying to figure out if Dan is excited or despondent. He is sensitive to Misty's feelings. This is not a time for riffing, not yet. He tells her he wants the job, and one of them would have had to quit anyway. That now they can stay together. Misty is not sure about moving. The mood is somber. She suggests that they could try a long distance relationship. Dan tries to lighten things up. "You like phone sex." Misty smiles. "Yes, and I like the real thing better." They hug and hold each other.

Jan is not happy. She feels that she deserves that job. She is the only one who has a degree, and management has always been her goal. Over drinks they commiserate. Jan, in spite of her disappointment, wishes Dan well. Ben gives Dan a dig when he asks if Misty is now single. Misty says, "He's soon to be a parent," and everyone ribs Dan. They finish coffee on a light note and Dan heads into the boss's office to accept the promotion. While in the office the boss asks him if he was having second thoughts. He explains that Jan is senior sales, and she taught him everything he knows. The boss has a surprise for Jan as well.

Jan follows Dan into the boss's office. She is told that, with her kids, it didn't seem like a good move for her, that she is being considered for Sales Manager of *this* office, if he is promoted to regional sales as is expected. Clearly the success of this office is reverberating throughout the company and furthering the careers of many of them. Is that how you expected this section to end? Did you expect that they would break up into infighting? Well, I tried to play with that expectation.

This group goes on meeting for drinks whenever Dan is in town for business, or they are at a conference. I occasionally join them when I am in town. As sales managers, Dan and Jan speak and laugh often. Cathy is promoted to Senior Sales and Misty is her chief competitor for weekly high sales. They broke up the group and made several of them managers. It's not all that bad. I hope to eventually work with all six offices. I sell more books, and it is ripe for the sequel: *Improv for Dating*.

In Summary

People who already practice these principles, whether having learned them, as I have, from improv, or have merely deduced them over time, usually hang out among others who are fun conversationalists. Chances are if you were one of the aforementioned, you were probably not invited back to parties. This journey began for me when I tried to save several friends from being politely un-invited to parties and events. I spelled out the rules: Several were like Zach, talked too much and used conversation as a place to vent. Some were just un-interesting when they weren't talking about their latest project; they rarely added to the group conversation. People like them are conversation killers. Do not be a conversation killer! Let the conversation live. Breathe life into it by finding the game within the conversation.

Conversation in business is about making an im-pression, leaving an impression. What could be better for a sales exec than a lasting impression that makes clients want to talk to you? What greater a leader can you be if your staff want to rally around you, enjoy you? Management is easy with someone who cares. Most business deals are about relationships, not nuts and bolts. The best deal does not often win the contract, the best relationship does. Build rapport! People want to do business with people whose company they enjoy.

Part Five: Specific Business Situations

Now that we have learned how to riff in social situations let's apply our skills to particular business situations.

Elevators and other situations with new clients

In most social situations where you are with a group of people that you do not know well, you should engage. Most people stick to themselves in these situations. Try to introduce a mildly provocative thought. Keep it simple, and it helps if it is self-deprecating. See if you can't get everyone to lighten up a little bit. You will be remembered, and the next time you see that person or those persons, you will undoubtedly revisit your last little riff. You are building rapport with co-workers or servers, doormen and valets or whomever. Leave a lasting impression and you will be treated as a friend the next time you interact with these people. I travel through the same airports every week and you can be sure that every person I interact with is very helpful; the TSA staff know me well. This rapport may rub off when you are with clients. If everyone likes you and has something funny to say when they see you, you are becoming popular. People like to do business with popular people.

Have you ever been standing waiting for an elevator where everyone who exits is laughing together even though they have never met? It does not take much to build rapport. A good laugh is a good start.

Sometimes a stupid question *is* a good way to lighten up a heavy room. "Why do the doors open to the sides and not up and down?" Is a good self-deprecating icebreaker. Someone is bound to point out that the elevator would have to be twelve feet tall before they realized that you were kidding.

"Should a man exit an elevator before a women or after?" It is a provocative question. The etiquette answer is a man should *enter* first and lady should *exit* first. Regardless, try and provoke conversation.

"Do you like to stand at the front or the back of an elevator?" You would be surprised how many people actually have a preference. You might learn something about your client as well.

"Why is the trap door on the ceiling and not the floor?" "I'll press my own buttons, thank you very much." "So, who has the most expensive shoes?" If you have been reading you can already see where each of the above riffs might go. In these situations a question helps to get people out of their heads. Again, use questions wisely.

Often the ride up to the meeting or the pick-up at the airport is the first real time you have with the client.

Getting a laugh is a sure way to break the ice and give you a leg up on everyone else. Then keep the riff going. You and only you both share it. They are in your club now. Your foot is in the elevator door, letting them in.

Travel

Traveling is a good time to practice riffing around people where the stakes are relatively low. That is to say making a good impression is not as important to a complete stranger as it is to a client. As in the above elevator discussion, you may need to initiate conversation in these situations. You obviously have one thing you share with the other travelers and that is travel itself. We have all had conversations about various airlines and their schedules, blackout dates, etc. Again look to reverse expectation. Say something provocative, that is to say provoke conversation. Reverse the expectation that all people ever talk about in airports is travel, sports, and where the nearest power source is.

There are also times that you are stuck next to

someone who is a talker. It might pass the time, but at the expense of everyone else seated around you. Knowing the various personality types is helpful. Play a game with yourself to see if you can spot them. Eventually the thing that you share is that they talk too much. When that is the one thing you share then that is the time to mention it. See if they can learn to diffuse criticism. Yeah, good luck. I suggest carrying this book around, hopefully they will read it and stop talking.

The First Meeting

That leads me to the first meeting – getting your foot in the door. Or the icebreaker as it is called. Your goal should be to loosen up an otherwise stiff situation as soon as you can. If this is going to be a successful meeting you will have to go from stiff tight conversation to joking about the merits of raising a girl versus a boy, or college vs pro football, or blades vs cavity back irons.

What you are looking for is some common ground. Are they football fans? Golfers? Music buffs?

Parents? Let's hope you have done your research, but, unfortunately, so have all your competitors. Customer relations management is important, not because it reminds you of who that person is but that it reminds you what everyone else already knows. In this case you should avoid things that are common knowledge. Everyone knows that your Mr. Smith is a USC Trojans fan, has two sons in college, and plays to a zero handicap. Avoid bringing these things up, nay, guide them to bring them up themselves.

As I write this there is public discussion about unionizing college football. Knowing Mr. Smith is a USC booster, bringing this conversation up might be a way to lead him to loosen up and talk USC football. Don't ask if he is a USC fan – if you went to USC then by all means bring it up. But if not say, "I hear you are a Trojans fan." That is going to be too "on-the-nose." Try to find a way into something the other person wants to talk about. If you spend the next fifty-five minutes of your hour laughing about football, agreeing to disagree where need be, you have already closed the deal. All that's left is the paperwork. Let that other person lead into it, though. Try not to be "on the nose." I'll talk more on that later.

In personal meetings pay attention to their attire, their energy. Try first to find things that you have in common. The cut of a suit, wing tips. Rubber- vs leather-soled shoes, but not weather or traffic. It can be anything, as you have seen a riff can start anywhere. Expand and heighten, find the game within the game, agree.

Try to leave the impression on everyone that you are a person they want to see again, that they cannot wait to see again, that they laugh with every time the two of you are together. Remember, a business relationship is a relationship first and last.

"Gosh, it was such a pleasure meeting you. I just can't wait till we can get together again!"

Closing the Deal

Just as in riffing, closing the deal is about leading them to it. But if time is running out I suggest a few closes that are good for coming out of a conversational riff and getting the point.

The first is the best: **ask for it**. "I have to get back to work."

"Yeah, me too. How many cases do you need?"

The second is the **order form close**. "Are you still at Blankety Blank Way? And that is six cases and three boxes?"

The third is the **final objection close**. "So, let me get this straight, your final objection is the shipping fee? If I can get my manager to approve free shipping then we are a go?" If they say yes, call them back with a condition. "OK, she said she would do it if you ordered the full gross." This close is especially good for people who talk you around forever without placing an order. Watch out for these; the cleverer you become the more time people will want to spend with you.

The Benjamin Franklin is good when you have a competitor that they like. Start by listing all the benefits of buying your product. Help them out with this. "Price, convenience, color selection, check, easy returns, check, and don't forget the perks: order twelve cases in one year and you get a free weekend in Cancun on us." Then when they list your competitor, shut up. They'll say, "We have been doing business for years." You say, "That's important." They say, "I was at Sam's (the other salesman's) wedding." You say, "I'm sure that meant a lot to him." They will invariably begin to repeat themselves. "We *have* been with them a long time." Now you may want to hit them with your list again. "Yeah, and look how much it has been costing you," as a way to mention price. "Yeah, and they are half-way across the country," as a way to mention your point about convenience. And so on. Let them dig a hole that they cannot get out of without sounding like a fool. Let's face it, if you are any good at sales you already know all the classic closes. Use the ones that come best out of the good rapport you have built while riffing during the sales call.

Opening and Closing a Meeting

A business meeting can have many forms and take place in many venues. Most business deals are hatched over lunch or cocktails. These social situations are different because everyone has an agenda. Whether you are selling or buying, your rapport with your counterpart is an important factor in whether you consummate the deal.

You should spend as much time as you need to build this rapport, and the best way to do that is to laugh together. Go to the circumstances. If you are in the position of having a short time to impress a client you must not force the issue. Wait for them to say something about the circumstances. Then, *Expand and Heighten.* "What is the deal with these polyester napkins? They don't absorb anything," a grumpy client said to me once. Agree: "They do fold into nice pirate hats." After a gentle laugh, expand and heighten your own riff. "I never know whether we should wear them or put them on our laps." That could lead to an "Aye, aye, mate," to the waiter. An "Arrrgh," as you cut through the tough piece of meat. Now you both have a pirate riff going.

You may think that the worst thing that can happen is that your choice in restaurants is called into question, but in actuality, turning around a criticism is the easiest way to find humor, and turn around a client. Agree! *Yes, and.* If the meeting opens with that comment, you probably have some digging to do. So cut to the chase: "Yes, you are right, and you are right to have concerns about my investment opportunity. But unfortunately I can't fix the restaurant …"

Look for places to lead into the inevitable business conversation. Look for segues both in and out. When the business part of the discussion has concluded bring back the pirate riff to close. Remember to ask,

"Do I have to tap my heels together, or do we have a deal?" as you pay the check. Keep the riff going even during the business. Use phrases like, "Walk the plank" or "Hard astern" or even, if you can *sell* it, "shiver me timbers."

But know when it is not working or when it has passed. Watch your counterpart closely, listen, expand and support their position. Regardless of whether you really agree with them.

Running a Meeting

Almost everyone wants to win, or champion, his or her own ideas. Do your homework, that is, think about what Zach is going to say about the new computers. Etc. See the riff coming before it happens.

In reality, you should already have the meeting sorted out before the meeting. You should have spoken to everyone in advance. You should know everyone's agenda and the meeting should be short and sweet.

Yeah, right.

Start by steering the nervous energy to something off topic, or dragging the lack of energy up. Laughter works here as well. Make a bet on the over and under of the time. That is a fun agenda. My money's on the over with Cathy in the room. The point is to call people out on their own foibles. As long as you call yourself out more. You may find that running a meeting is the same as meeting one on one with a client, that is to say, the more time that is spent riffing the easier the nitty-gritty stuff seems to go by.

Opening and Closing

By now we should understand what *opening with a joke* means. It does not mean to tell a joke. It means to find something funny to say that is in the circumstance. It can be arranged, set up, or at least thought about. But it should not be an anecdote unless it is immediate.

Brainstorming

Brainstorming is, by definition, without judgment. Sound familiar? Riffing is without judgment. *Expand and Heighten* is at the heart of all brainstorming sessions. Let go of your ego. A famous producer once said to me, "No one remembers whose idea it was except the person whose idea it was, so stop fighting for your idea." *Expand and heighten* someone else's idea. One of the greatest gifts that come with these skills is that you make other people look better. I cannot think of a single quality that I would rather have. Wouldn't you want to associate with someone who makes you look good?

If you have been working on your conversational skills you should already understand that.

Most people follow their personality types. There is Jan who thinks that everyone should have a say. There's Cathy and Dan who think that no one else has anything important to say. There is Misty who has nothing to say. Every meeting eventually boils down to everyone's gravitating to his or her true self. Cathy will not shut up and stop asking question so everyone can get back to work. We all know this person. Dan thinks talking more will win his point, and so on.

Communicating Up and Down

We all have a tendency to spend less time riffing with subordinates. But they are the ones who have your back – at least you hope they do. To insure they do you must use the same care and energy to riff with them as you do with your superiors and clients. There isn't a conversation you should have that you are not at some point picking up on a riff. The seriousness of the situation only means that you need to riff a lot less and have serious conversation. But the person who is suffering can appreciate a good riff in a dire situation such as a client in the hospital or the death of a co-worker.

Sucking up to the boss is basically making them look good. Work on the self-deprecating humor as Zach managed to do in his meeting with the boss over the transition of the shipping department. Admit in advance your own and your work's deficiencies. Then expand on that: "Math is not my strong suit; you should see my tax return."

"My room is always cluttered; ask my wife."

"My wife says I'll be late for my own funeral."

"I was late for my wedding."

"I need someone else to shop for me."

"Copy machines hate me, and don't ask about coffee makers!"

Agree, agree, and agree to your superiors. They are always right.

Meeting a famous person

A first meeting with a famous person can be daunting. You obviously know more about them than they do about you. Just as in the previous discussion try to let them bring those things up. I recently met a famous movie star in a social situation. We had a mutual friend. My friend had told me that this star was once a world-class motocross racer. I had not known that nor was it public knowledge. I myself had raced motocross so I knew it was something we had in common, something to riff on.

In my particular situation I had a pitch for him; I had some business to propose. Now, as is often the case he had no idea who I was and had no reason to hear my pitch. If I had gone right into it he would have balked immediately and told me to call his agent; he was with his children and their nanny. The first thing I did is walk right up and introduce myself. My friend had always called him Mr. Wilson although they were the same age. I introduced myself by my first name; he shook my hand and said, "Sam," not Samuel as the media called him, not Mr. Wilson. Since he introduced himself as Sam, Sam is what I called him.

My plan was to get him to talk about this house above a hill and about practicing on his motorcycle when he was younger. My first move was to introduce myself to his sons. They were clever and engaging. I suggested that we throw the football around and he stopped me. Telling me that American Football was too dangerous. He didn't want them playing it. He added that rugby was played without all the pads and had relatively few concussion related injuries. Not knowing the first thing about rugby I was in trouble. I had offended him and had to listen to his rant about the subject. I sauntered away defeated, not a good time to bring up my pitch.

I regrouped. I found his other son in the house trying to play my friend's drum set (my friend was renting Mr. Wilson's house). He came in and was pleased to see his younger son enjoying himself on the drum kit. He asked me if I played – now I had my opening. I said no, that I no longer played and told him an anecdote about how my father had always regretted buying me a drum kit when I was young. I told Mr. Wilson that I had always wanted a motorcycle. Now, both my parents were wary of the dangers but also fed up with the constant banging on the drums. They made me a deal: they would help me buy a new motorcycle if I sold the drums. And that, I told him, was why I no longer played.

He laughed, understanding young boys the way he did. And then proceeded to tell me a long anecdote about how he used to lead highway police on long chases across Australia when he was younger, noting that there was no radio on the police bikes. I shot back with, "By the time I was a teenager they had helicopters! Try outrunning one of those!" He laughed again and I spent the rest of the BBQ laughing and talking bikes. We built such a rapport that no one else could get into a conversation with him. No one else was in on our riff. We became friends from that afternoon on. So when I mentioned to him that I had a great idea that might suit him he was excited to hear it. He said I could send it to him directly without having to go through his management. I pitched the deal and got the project on. We have worked together ever since.

Be smart, try to find something that you share. Let them start to lead the conversation. Build rapport before you leap into business discussions.

In Summary

So, to summarize, good conversation is about expanding and heightening what is between you and the other people in the room. There is a time for a good yarn and there are people who love to hear about your vacation, but keep it to a minimum. Follow the rules of good conversation. Avoid questions like, "How was your weekend?" Don't start conversations with "I." "I think Kennedy was killed by the CIA and here is why … Blah, blah, blah." A negation has many forms. Do not negate. Remember *Yes, and...*

Expand and Heighten!

Praise for Robin and *Improv for Executives* –

I wish I had read this before I moved to England

– Amir Hosseinpour – President, Fitness Concepts

Robin is a lot of fun on the golf course.

– Shane Hutton – Arcana Academy Advertising

Wish I had read this before I became a producer.

– Jennifer C. Wolfe – Private Producer

Robin is lots of laughs on a date.

– Robin's girlfriend

This Shit doesn't work.

– Colin Gibbons – Music Manager

Best book I ever read.

– Sean Mahoney – Robin's Publicist

Robin G Brown, relaxing in his Southern California home and thinking about his next book, *Improv for Dating*.

About the Author

R G Brown has a bachelor's degree from Western Illinois University in business and a master's degree from the University of Southern California in theater. He is an alumnus of the Second City Training center and performed with the Improv Olympic in Chicago where he was directed by Del Close. He later taught Improvisation for the Theater at the Stella Adler Conservatory, West.

He has spent a lifetime teaching anyone who will listen how to be more comfortable in social and business situations, using the basic principles of improvisation. This quest has led him to lecturing at business conferences and ultimately working with private companies in order to help their employees become better in all business situations.

NOTES

NOTES

Advance praise for *People Development...*

"*Developing people is the most rewarding part of being a leader. A focus on helping people, guiding people to new heights, not only brings a sense of self-fulfillment, but it also creates a high-performing team comprised of employees who want to stay working for you! But it takes an informed and organized approach. In this book, Jim provides both the theoretical foundation and real-life examples to help you think more deeply about how you will go about building your people. He has built a concise blueprint that sums up what took me decades to learn. If you care about your employees, you must read this book.*"

—*Jay Held, Retired Vice President of Training and Development*

"*Jim Bohn hits it out of the park again! People Development: The Best Part of Leading a Team is chock-full of thought-provoking insights, relevant tools, and practical implications! I picked the book up and couldn't put it down. Jim's years of leadership experience and expertise in managing and motivating team members really shine throughout this book. A must read for any leader looking to continually elevate the performance of their teams! I can't wait to share it with my colleagues.*"

—Kim Thelen, Senior Director, Global Account
    Operations, CBRE

"*This book is very timely. There is a quiet desperation for guidance and support for the manager, the contributor, and the organization!*"

—Elizabeth Thelen, Executive Director, Whitewater University
    Technology Park